Wisdom on How to Live Life

Transforming Earth into Heaven

Dr. Tommy S. W. Wong

Dedicated to

my parents, Wong Sze Fong and Woo En Yueh

my parents-in-law, Sum Chip Shing and Ko Luk Ying

my darling wife, Christina

and my wonderful sons, Alston, Lester and Hanson

Acknowledgement

I like to thank the Great Spirit for selecting me as an instrument in authoring this book for the benefit of mankind.

Table of Contents

Chapter 1

Introduction

Humans being the most intelligent species and having lived on Earth for thousands of years, we are yet nowhere near to a life of peace, love, joy and harmony. This book contains a hypothetical story of a young man, Tom, who had conversations with two gurus, Dick and Harry. Guru Dick epitomizes someone from a worldly society who emphasized on the importance of money and power. Guru Harry epitomizes someone from a spiritual society who offered an alternative way of living which can lead to peace, love, joy and harmony.

In the first conversation, Guru Dick expounded his worldly wisdom on:

(1) what is good about money,
(2) what are the five easiest ways to make money,
(3) what are the relationships between money, power, law and god, and
(4) what is one great human weakness.

1

In the second conversation, Guru Harry expounded his spiritual wisdom on:

(1) why there is no need to worry,
(2) why peace is better than happiness as a goal in life,
(3) how to live in peace and equanimity,
(4) how to live with pleasure and without pain,
(5) how to live without fear,
(6) how to live without disappointment,
(7) how to live without struggle,
(8) how to live without sufferings,
(9) how to live without loneliness,
(10) how to be empowered in life,
(11) which type of attachment can bring bliss,
(12) which relationship can last forever,
(13) how to appraise world leaders,
(14) what society should be focused on,
(15) what is the objective of education,
(16) what is true charity,
(17) what is miracle,
(18) what is karma,
(19) why it is important to get the "right" beliefs,
(20) why reincarnation is important,
(21) why there is no need to grieve,
(22) what are the differences between man-made and divine laws,

(23) what are the important spiritual concepts,

(24) how to become divine, and

(25) how to transform Earth into heaven.

On other aspects of life, the two gurus offered contrasting views on:

(1) what is success in life,

(2) what are the purposes of life,

(3) how to enjoy life,

(4) how to achieve freedom in life,

(5) how to behave in life,

(6) how to live with morality,

(7) what are the major problems in the world,

(8) why not working for a living,

(9) how parents should be treated,

(10) how to decide whether to get married,

(11) how children should be treated,

(12) how to select friends,

(13) how to improve the education system, and

(14) how to bring peace on Earth.

Through these conversations, young Tom is better prepared and becomes wiser on how to live his life.

Wisdom on how to live life

Chapter 2

Conversation with Guru Dick

How are you, Guru Dick?

Not very well, Tom. The doctor told me that I only have a few more days to live. All the things I've accumulated in my life, I now have to leave them behind. Anyway, it is good of you to come to see me.

Do you want to talk or would you prefer to take a rest?

We can talk. I like to talk.

What would you like to talk about?

Anything. I'm old enough to be able to talk about anything. What would you like to talk about?

How about we talk about life?

That is a great idea because I'm near the end of my life and I had a great life.

Do you think you had a successful life?

Of course, you see how much money I've made.

Are you happy?

Of course, you see how much money I've made.

Is life just about making money?

Not quite, it is about money and power. You see if you have money, then you have power. You will also have security and freedom. That is why it is important to have money.

What else is good about money?

If you have money, people will look up to you and will "bow" to you and that includes government ministers. Once I donated a lot of money to a university in a foreign country, and even the President of that country had dinner with me. Once you have money, you can feel secure because if anything happens, money can help you out. No doubt money can't do everything, but then is there anything that can. If you have money, you can also gain power and that includes political power. And the best part about money is that you can have freedom. You can live wherever you like. You can do whatever you like and that includes bending the law. Oh heck, with lots of money, you can even break the law. No, with lots and lots of money, you are the law. Wouldn't you say that is "real" freedom?

Well, I see your point, but money can't cure your illness and can't save your life?

Yes that is true, but because I have lots of money, I can hire the best doctors, use the best equipment and the best medicine. So I have the best chance to survive. Money can do wonders.

If money is so good, what is the best way to make money?

The best way to make money is defined by "efficiency" which is maximum output with minimum input.

What does that mean?

It means that you get maximum monetary reward by doing minimum amount of work.

How can that be? I thought a fair day's pay for a fair day's work.

This is what bosses tell their workers. It is to brainwash them so that they can get maximum output with minimum pay.

So how can we be "efficient"?

Okay, the easiest way is by inheritance. You see if you are born in a rich family, and they give you a pot of gold, then you got gold by doing nothing. Isn't this efficient? But there is a catch.

What is the catch?

The catch is that you must behave the "right" way, so that they will give you gold. You see what is the use of being born in a rich family and not getting gold?

Well I'm not born in a rich family, is there another way?

The second easiest way is through power.

How does that work?

You see power and money go hand in hand. Like I told you, if you have money, you get power. Well, the converse is also true. If you have power, you get money.

That sounds good.

Extremely! If you want to get money through power, you must get the best power.

What is the best power?

Political power, and you must get the best political power.

What is the best political power?

Absolute political power.

You mean dictatorship?

Well dictatorship is one form of absolute political power, but actually it is not the best type.

Why?

People usually resent dictators. So dictators can't stay long. It is worse when dictators step down because people seek revenge.

What happens with revenge?

Whatever privileges they enjoyed during their period of power, they usually have to pay it back after they have stepped down, and most of them suffer for the rest of their lives.

So dictatorship is not the best absolute political power, is there a better type?

Yes, and it is called pseudo-democracy.

Wow, that is a new word. What does that mean?

Pseudo-democracy means it looks like a democracy on the outside, like having elections, but in reality it is not a democracy.

How can that be, an election is an election and in the election, people decide, right?

That is a "normal" election. What if a ruling party for whatever reason happens to have an overwhelming majority and then they modify the election system so that it is completely in their favor. With such a system, how can the opposition stand a chance? So, what can the people choose? What can the people decide?

Wouldn't the opposition object?

They may, but since their political power is so limited, their objection is quite useless.

Wouldn't the people object?

They might, but they can be easily pacified.

How?

Set some policies which favor the rich and powerful. In this way, you win their support. After that, what can the poor and powerless do?

Look after the rich and don't care about the rest.

Well, to be on the safe side, we can also offer something to the poor, like peanuts to monkeys.

You mean people are monkeys.

Well, let me put it this way. Have you been to a circus?

Yes.

What happens when a trainer instructs a monkey to jump, and the monkey jumps?

The trainer rewards the monkey with peanuts.

Bravo! In human society, the same thing happens except the terminologies change.

What do you mean?

The term "jump" is called "job", "peanuts" is called "salary", "trainer" is called "boss", and "monkey" is called "worker".

So workers are monkeys?

If you look at their salaries, some of them are real peanuts, right? Not even enough for monkeys.

Well, at least you are in favor of giving to the poor.

I'm not in favor of giving to the poor or anybody. I'm not really giving because real giving means you give something and expect nothing in return. In this case, I'm giving them something and expect them not to protest. It is really "protection money".

After pacifying the rich and the poor, are we in safe hands?

We are very safe because humans have one great weakness.

What is that?

Everyone for himself. That is why we must divide them into groups and give each group a little something.

Then?

They will fight among themselves.

Divide and rule.

Precisely! An age old strategy which has kept "bad" government in power for decades.

What do you call this type of system?

A one-party system and this is the best type of absolute power.

Why?

Because you gained power through elections, so they can't call you dictators, and yet you have absolute power.

Then, what happens?

After you have absolute power, life is easy. You can decide how much you want to get paid.

Okay.

And you don't really have to work. Wouldn't you call that "efficient"?

Very efficient. But what happens if I'm not born in a rich family and don't have political power?

Then, the third way is to become a CEO, chief executive officer.

That sound like a lot of work. Also a CEO has to make the organization perform, otherwise he is out.

That is the "normal" CEO. But you can look for organizations where CEOs don't have to perform. These organizations can lose a huge amount of money and yet the CEOs are rewarded.

Really?

Better still, they can blame the inept performance on their subordinates and fire them, while they collect their big fat performance bonus.

How come they can get performance bonus while they are not performing?

Privileges of CEOs.

But we shouldn't take what we don't deserve, right?

If they willingly give, then you can willingly take.

But it is still not right, right?

Who says so?

My higher consciousness.

Then, tell your higher consciousness that it is alright to take, the more the better.

Who will tell my higher consciousness?

Your lower consciousness?

I see. Now is there another way to make lots of money?

Yes there is a fourth way, but in this, one needs to do some work.

Oh great, at last there is a way to work for a living.

My young Tom, don't ever think of working for a living. It is too slow and you will make very little money. You will have to struggle for your entire life and by the time you retire, you won't have enough.

Then, what is the fourth way to make lots of money?

The fourth way is to become a banker.

How does that work?

You come up with some investment products, package them as attractive as you can and hide all the details.

Then?

Misrepresent the products so that your customers will think that they can make lots of money. In reality, of course they will lose and you will gain and that is the idea.

Isn't this unethical, a devious way of making money?

There is no right or wrong way of making money. Whichever way you can make the fastest and the largest amount of money is the best way.

Wouldn't the government step in to curb this type of products or worse still, penalize those who come up with this type of products?

My friend, governments have power, and bankers are rich. The rich and powerful always stand on the same side.

To suppress the poor and the powerless.

Welcome to the real world!

So the rich get richer, and the poor get poorer.

Yes, let's make the income gap wider.

What happens if the investment products are sold to an old and poor retiree?

This is the name of the game. Some will win and some will lose. Anyway, if this old and poor retiree holds on to the money, it will not grow very fast right. So it is much better for us bankers to hold on to the money and make it grow faster.

How will this old person live, if he loses all his savings?

That is his problem. We are here to make us richer – the richer the better, and by whatever means. Remember this young Tom, money and power are the two goals in life.

Sounds like you are obsessed with money and power.

Of course, so should you. They are the only criteria defining whether you are a success or not.

How about love and kindness?

What about them? Look at it this way; have you seen any kind person becoming rich?

I can't say I have.

You see.

It sounds to me you are quite immoral?

Don't talk to me about "morality". This is one of the biggest problems on Earth.

How come you say morality is a problem?

Morality leads people to sufferings. Isn't it a problem if you live like a beggar and suffer for the rest of your life?

Well, I would rather be poor and moral, than rich and immoral.

Young Tom, this kind of thinking will lead you nowhere. It will not do you or the world any good. You see the world needs rich people so that they can do good.

But the rich people don't do good?

Never mind what the rich do. Tell me what can the poor do?

I see what you mean.

Also being rich is not immoral, right? So means of getting rich can't be immoral.

How about for the bankers to come up with investment products that can really make money for their customers, so it is a win-win solution?

Don't be stupid. If bankers know how to make money through investment, then they don't have to work, right?

You mean they are not here to serve the customers?

Young Tom, get this into your head. We are not here to serve anybody. We are here to serve ourselves.

Self-service.

Anyway, since your customers are giving you money, isn't much easier just to pocket that money? Do you know how difficult it is to make money through investment?

How difficult?

It is so difficult that it is not worth doing. So it is much easier just to pocket your customers' money.

Sounds like you are committed to be rich and powerful and achieve them by whatever means.

Yes, Tom, I'm glad that you finally got the idea. Afterall, we are only committed to achieve our goals in life.

Apart from morality, what else do you think is a major problem in the world today?

Poor people especially those who are poor and old.

I thought the major problems today are terrorists and global warming.

These are opportunities, my friend!

You mean terrorists and global warming are your friends?

Why not? They are golden opportunities to make big money.

I thought we have to spend big money to solve these problems.

Exactly! If somebody is prepared to spend big money, then it is an opportunity to make big money.

How?

You see the easiest way to get people to spend big money is through fear.

Really?

You see how much is spent on armed forces and insurances.

A lot, a lot of money.

Why?

Because of fear?

Precisely! Both terrorists and global warming also produce fear. In fact, big fear. So they are sure to spend big money.

Can we get back to the major problem mentioned by you which is poor people?

Sure.

You mean they are a problem because we need to help them?

No, no, no, young Tom. We don't help anybody. We are only here to take, the more the better.

So how can poor people be a problem?

They are a problem because they take in something and then return something less. So with them around, the world becomes poorer and poorer. And then the problem is worse for the old and poor because they have no economic value.

So what should we do with these people?

Since these people are consuming the world's resources and cannot pay back, the best way is to remove them.

What? To remove them, you mean to kill them. And then I thought it is the rich who are consuming the world's resources.

Yes, the rich are consuming the world's resources, but they pay for them. So what is the problem? Yes, to remove the poor means to end their lives.

Wow, how cruel? Isn't it inhumane to kill your fellow human beings?

Well, young Tom, if you look at the history of human beings, killing fellow human beings happens all the time. While murders are generally unacceptable to society, there are many other forms of killings that are not just acceptable but even glorified.

Such as?

Wars which can be on a global or at a local scale, in either case the countries involved usually glorify the mass killings. Terrorists who organize the terrorists' attacks usually glorify the mass killings. There are even legalized individual killings such as death penalty and euthanasia. These are also glorified by their respective societies.

But these killings are meant for the good of the world!

What I'm recommending is also for the good of the world.

Isn't it inhumane?

If you look at the lives of these old and poor people, they are so miserable and full of sufferings. I'll say it is very humane.

23

How about getting the rich to help the poor?

Ah aye, Tom, have you forgotten the goals of life? We are here to become rich and powerful. We are not here to help the poor or anybody. How can the rich give money to the poor? I mean who needs the money.

I thought it is the poor who need the money?

Yes, they need money only if they want to survive but now we are giving them something better. We are giving them a complete solution so that they don't need money anymore. We are helping them to solve their problem once and for all and till time immemorial.

Wow, you have a weird way of thinking.

No, no, no, my thinking is actually very rational. You see why are people poor? It is because when they take in certain number of dollars, they produce something less. On the other hand, when the rich take in certain number of dollars, they produce something more. So it is completely rational to channel all the money to the rich. In this way, everyone in this world will be rich, and there will be peace on Earth.

Amen!

Absolutely, it is the rich and powerful that are really doing good to the world. The poor are simply troublemakers. Remove them, and there'll be no more trouble.

Can we change the subject to education?

Sure, we all need a good education.

You mean you are in favor of a good education?

I'm in favor of all things good and beautiful.

That includes killing your fellow human beings?

We have discussed that before. It is good for the world.

What do you think of the present education system?

It is good but make it longer.

Some people already spend more than 20 years studying; you mean this is not long enough?

Yes, it is long but make it longer, the longer the better.

You mean to make it longer so that the students can learn more and be better equipped for the working world?

No, no, no, education has nothing to do with learning. It is a system to keep these young people away from the work place so that they don't compete with us.

So your idea of making the education system longer is only for your benefit?

No, it benefits all the people in the work place.

How about from the students point of view? Is the education system too long?

We don't consider things from the others point of view. We are here to protect our own interests.

Does everybody think like you?

No, only successful leaders.

You mean only "successful" leaders.

I mean truly successful leaders.

Do all "successful" leaders think like you?

Name one who doesn't.

I see your point.

You should also see that there are people dying of hunger on our planet.

Yes, I do.

This problem has been around for many generations.

Yes.

Why do you think the world is in such a state?

I thought the problem is too large and complicated. So it takes time to sort it out.

But the problem has been around for generations, and actually there is sufficient food for all. Don't you think we should have sorted it out by now?

Yes, one would imagine so.

So why isn't it sorted out?

Because nobody is doing it?

Right, because all leaders are only looking after their own interests.

They are?

There is one more sobering thought.

What is it?

Are the leaders really performing when there is still hunger on Earth?

Are they?

You see for the survival of human body, food is the most basic need.

Most basic.

So an easy way to tell the performance of leaders is to see whether there is hunger at the bottom stratum of society.

Look at the bottom and not the top.

Is there?

There is.

So?

So, how can we change them?

Ha, young man, listen carefully. Humans are one of the few species who will kill their own kind. With many other species, they may fight each other but they won't kill their own kind.

You mean humans are crueler than animals?

You can also see how many humans have been killed by fellow humans.

Far too many.

And it is still happening today.

Yes, throughout the entire human history.

Humans are the cruelest species on Earth. It is in their nature, so how can we change them?

I was told that humans are divine.

Yes, there is a more accurate word to describe humans which also starts with "d" but it is not divine.

What is it?

Demonic.

You mean humans are demons?

Just look at the world today.

Yes, I'm looking.

Anyway, who told you that humans are divine?

A divine being.

Is he rich?

I don't think so because I don't think he keeps money.

Does he have political power?

I think he has divine power but not political power.

Ha you see, never listen to somebody who is not rich and has no political power.

So you are saying humans are not divine and there is no love in humans?

You better be clear on this or you will have a hard life. You must be ruthless, fight and grab for whatever you want, or you will get nothing.

Kill or be killed.

Exactly.

What do you think of religion?

Great job!

You mean great teaching?

No, I mean great job because you can make easy money from religion.

I thought religion is about teaching people to be good, and not about making money.

You look at how many people have become rich by being religious leaders.

Rich and powerful.

Super rich and powerful!

How about the teaching?

Never mind the teaching. Earlier I mentioned four easy ways of making money. Actually, religion can beat three of them.

Which three?

Politicians, CEOs and bankers.

How come?

All these three have to deliver in this lifetime.

And for the religious leaders?

All their promises are for the afterlife, so actually they don't have to deliver at all.

But if they don't deliver, God will punish them.

Who says there is God?

Religious leaders.

So they claim they know God?

Well, that is why they are religious leaders, right?

I'm not so sure.

So do you believe in God?

I know God.

Wow, that is good. Tell me about God.

Money is god, power is god. And I've money and power, so I'm god.

I thought God is not about money and power. It is about love.

So they tell you.

Yes, all the time.

Do you believe them?

You mean it is not true?

Like I said, whatever they tell you, they don't have to deliver.

What about family?

What about it?

Is it good to get married and have a family?

Only if it will make you rich.

How about parents?

Yes, what about them?

Should we look after them?

If they promise to give you lots of money, maybe you have to.

Otherwise?

Dump them.

Dump them?

Yes, if you have siblings, pass them to your siblings. If you don't have siblings, pass them to your relatives. If you don't have siblings and relatives, pass them to an old folks home.

You mean we shouldn't look after them?

Do you know how much is involved in looking after your old parents?

How much?

It is a 24-hour job. Anything can happen to these old folks anytime, so you have to be on standby all the time. So you can't do much traveling, and you can't have long holidays.

But we still have to look after them, right?

Who says so?

My higher consciousness.

Then, tell your higher consciousness that it is alright to dump them.

Who'll tell my higher consciousness?

Your lower consciousness?

I see.

And looking after your parents is not for one or two years. What happens if your parents live to 100 years?

We should then thank God for blessing our parents for living such a long life.

Yes, you should also thank God for your imprisonment which can be 10 years or longer?

Imprisonment?

Yes, once you are committed to look after your parents, there are many things you can't do, just like in a prison.

But isn't it better to serve our parents than doing all the other things?

It is better to serve yourself, remember self-service, make money, enjoy life and be happy.

But our parents won't be happy?

That is their problem. We promised them nothing when we were born.

But looking after our parents may encourage our children to look after us next time?

They also promise you nothing when they are born.

How about friends?

Yes, we need them.

We do?

Yes, we need connections to be rich and powerful.

So what kind of friends should we keep?

Must you ask? The rich and powerful, of course.

But they are not genuine?

Never mind. As long as the money and power are genuine, it is good enough.

Guru Dick, is there anything else you would like to talk about?

Well, it has been a long chat. Maybe I'll take a rest now.

Guru Dick, maybe I won't have a chance to see you again before you go.

That is alright, Tom.

May you rest in peace, Guru Dick!

How can I be at peace when I'm going to lose all my money and power?

Well, thank you for all the worldly wisdom! I'm sure what you have said is right because you are considered a shining success in our society.

Goodbye, Tom!

Goodbye, Guru Dick!

Wisdom on how to live life

Chapter 3

Conversation with Guru Harry (Part 1)

How are you, Guru Harry?

I'm very well, Tom.

I thought the doctor said that you only have a few more days to live.

Yes, that is true. But that only means I'll leave my body in a few days' time.

You mean you are not worried about dying?

Well, dying means the soul is separated from the body but the soul will continue to live while the body is left behind. You know we are souls and not bodies, so why should I worry?

Do you want to talk or would you prefer to take a rest?

We can talk. I like to talk.

What would you like to talk about?

Anything. I'm old enough to be able to talk about anything. What would you like to talk about?

How about we talk about life?

That is a great idea because I'm near the end of my present incarnation and I had a great life.

Do you think you had a successful life?

Depends on how you define success. By my definition, I'll say I had a successful life.

Are you happy?

I would say I'm more at peace.

What is your definition of success?

A successful life is a life in which you have done good to others.

I thought life is about getting things for ourselves?

Who told you that?

Society leaders.

You mean they actually tell you that?

Well they may or may not have said it, but they certainly practice it.

Action speaks louder than words.

Exactly!

There are many misguided souls on our planet.

Is that why the world is in such a state?

The world is like our home. It depends on the people living in it and what they do to it.

We certainly don't look after our planet.

You can say that again.

We certainly don't look after our planet.

Well said. If we don't look after our home, it will be in a mess, right? So why are you surprised that the world is in such a state?

Because the world is supposed to be looked after by leaders who are clever and smart.

But what happens if they are misguided?

You mean smart people can be misguided?

Smartness is a double-edge sword. It can heal or kill.

How can we heal the world?

By having the right concept.

What is the right concept?

We are souls and not bodies.

Guru Harry, this concept is not new. We have been told about this thousands of years ago. So why is the world still in such a mess?

Because many listen but few practice it.

You mean such a simple concept can help the world?

It can bring heaven to Earth.

Wow, we must talk about this. How does it work?

First, we must clarify the problems with identifying ourselves as bodies.

Our bodies can live and serve us for many years. So what are the problems?

After our bodies are born, they grow, then decay and finally die. Not everybody goes through all the processes; but once a body is born, its demise is guaranteed.

Okay, what you have described are the processes of life and death. They are pretty elementary.

Yes, they are. But the key is that the processes are governed by the laws of nature or divine laws; nobody, absolutely nobody can violate these laws.

I was told that the rich and powerful make the laws.

Who told you that?

The rich and powerful.

Well, they maybe able to make man-made laws, but the divine laws are made by the Divine.

Laws are laws, right? Who cares whether they are man-made or divine?

The wise will differentiate between them because there are hugh differences.

That is news to me. What are the differences?

The first is that since man-made laws are made by the men, they can be changed by men. So some man-made laws were made in the past and subsequently they were repealed by men. It means that man-made laws are not permanent. Some laws that we have today, come tomorrow they may be gone.

How about divine laws?

Divine laws do not change. They are the same forever and a day.

Sounds like small differences to me. We have to obey all laws, right?

Maybe, maybe not. Knowing the differences between man-made and divine laws will help you to decide.

Okay, what are the other differences?

The second major difference is in the enforcement. For man-made laws, you can actually violate them and still be free of punishment.

How come?

Because it depends on whether you get caught or not.

Is this why so many people break man-made laws?

Absolutely! For man-made laws, you can try your luck and take a chance.

What happens if you are unlucky?

First, you can blame the system; that is the "stupid" people who made such "stupid" laws. And then you can blame the "stupid" people who caught you. In fact, you will see them as culprits because they are the ones giving you trouble.

So, they are the troublemakers and we are never in the wrong?

Of course not. That is why man-made laws never really change one's behavior because it is a cat and mouse game.

Still, what happens when we get caught?

There is still a way out.

How?

For man-made laws, the punishment is given out by men.

That sounds logical, but how does that help us?

So, it is up to the man who is in a position to decide whether to give you punishment or not.

Surely he would apply the law equitably and fairly to everyone.

Have you heard of "one law for the rich" and "one law for the poor"?

So it is true. It is better to be rich and powerful.

Only for man-made laws.

How about divine laws?

Divine laws are laws of nature. So they don't need men to enforce them.

Wow, that is good, since nobody is enforcing them, we can happily break them?

I didn't say nobody is enforcing them. I said they are not enforced by men, but they are enforced by nature. So these laws are more potent because they are enforced everywhere all the time.

So, is there a chance of breaking them and not getting caught?

For divine laws, it is not a question of getting caught because it works on "action" and "reaction".

Can you elaborate?

The divine laws operate like a computer game. It has been programmed such that when you take one action, a reaction is bound to follow.

It is like "cause" and "effect".

Some call it "karma"!

But for some actions, we don't see the reaction.

That is only because we don't exactly know the divine laws. We don't really know what the reaction is meant to follow an action. Sometimes a reaction can be subtle or it can happen a long time after the action, so we can't recognize it.

So, is reaction a punishment?

Many think of it that way, and use it as a curse. Actually, reaction isn't a punishment, it is a feedback. It is a way of letting a person know how his action affects others. Sometimes a reaction can look like a punishment. Nonetheless, it is meant for the betterment of that person so that he will be wiser when he chooses his action next time round.

You mean we can repeat our actions, so we can repeat our mistakes?

In the realm of the divine, there are no mistakes. So in the computer game, we can repeat our actions and we can choose our actions freely.

You mean we are free to do whatever we like?

Within the programmed actions in the computer game.

And we suffer from all the programmed reactions?

We can enjoy them actually, like we enjoy computer games.

You know we can enjoy computer games because they are not real. Our lives are very real, and sometimes very painful. How can we enjoy them?

Have you heard of "Life is an illusion"?

Who told you that?

A divine being.

Is he rich?

A divine being doesn't amass wealth.

Does he have political power?

A divine being doesn't amass political power.

Then, he is pretty useless, isn't he? He is neither rich nor powerful.

But he knows and practices the divine truth.

What is that?

Life is an illusion.

Sounds like your divine being likes to talk in mumbo jumbo. How will that help us?

Like you said, we can enjoy computer games because they are not real. So if we believe life is not real, we can enjoy them too.

Your argument is pretty illusory. Anyway, let's get back to the divine laws.

Yes, back to the Divine.

So, how can divine laws help us?

You see with the divine laws, we can choose Action A which will be followed by Reaction B, or we can choose Action C which will be followed by Reaction D.

Okay!

Suppose we like Reaction B and not Reaction D, then the thing to do is when we take action next time, we choose Action A and not Action C.

That sounds pretty simple.

You see the Divine is teaching us to take "right" actions through a game of life.

Yes, the Divine is using a computer game to teach us the "right" behavior?

Correct.

If that is the case, why doesn't the Divine programme the game so that every human being will only do good?

If the game is programmed as you have suggested, are humans doing good out of "choice", or are they doing good out of "no choice"?

At least everyone is doing good.

Humans have to learn to do good out of "choice".

Why?

So that they can be divine.

I was told that humans are demonic and not divine.

Who told you that?

The rich and powerful.

51

Actually, they have a point. Humans can elevate themselves to become divine or degenerate to become demonic.

How can humans become divine?

Play the game and learn the "right" behavior.

Is that all?

It is all in the game.

Are there other differences between man-made and divine laws?

Yes, there is another major difference.

What is that?

What happens if the man-made laws say one thing and the divine laws say another?

You mean which ones should we follow?

I mean which ones do most people follow?

Divine laws, I would imagine.

Actually, it is the man-made laws you know.

How come?

One reason is that most people are more aware of the man-made laws than the divine laws because divine laws aren't exactly written in black and white.

In fact they are not written down at all.

Another reason is that most people are also more aware of the consequences of violating the man-made laws than the divine laws.

So, their regard for man-made laws is higher than divine laws.

Yes, but it should be the other way round.

Why?

Because when there are inconsistencies between man-made and divine laws, which ones do you think will prevail?

Divine laws?

Yes. Man think they are powerful but actually, who is more powerful?

The Divine.

Correct.

Okay, can we get back to the living and dying?

Yes, let's get back to the life and death issue.

I still don't see what is the problem as we live and then we die?

You are right; actually there is no problem with living and dying. The problem only comes when we identify ourselves with the body.

We can see the body. We can touch the body. Of course we identify ourselves with the body. What is wrong with that?

I've written an article on this. It is entitled "Who am I?" and can be found in Appendix A.

Yes, it is an interesting article. It shows how foolish it is to identify ourselves with the body.

Not only that, there is also a serious problem.

What is the problem?

If we identify ourselves with the body only, then we won't want the body to die because when the body dies, it is also the end of our beings.

Yes, that will be a problem, because we don't want to lose our beings.

Exactly! So the problem is after we are born, there is no way not to die.

Sounds like we are at a death trap. Is there any way out?

Humans are blessed beings. So how can the Divine lay a death trap for us?

But the body will die, and there is no way out!

Bingo, the secret is that we are not the body.

Oh yes, you have said that we are souls and not bodies.

Well remembered!

How will that help us?

If we identify ourselves as souls and our souls continue to live even after the death of our bodies, then well not be too concerned with the death of our bodies.

Okay, our souls live on after our bodies die.

Precisely!

Actually, how do we know this is true?

Here we are talking about spiritual concepts, and these concepts can't be proven using physical science.

So we won't know whether they are true?

Actually, whether they are true or not is not so important. A better way to look at these concepts is whether they help us in our daily lives.

How do we do that?

Let's take the concept that we are bodies.

Okay.

If we believe we are bodies and bodies only, we will do everything we can to keep our bodies going because if our bodies die, we also die.

Yes.

But there is a serious problem with this concept.

What is that?

It is impossible to keep our bodies going forever. It is against the laws of nature.

You mean it is wrong to see ourselves as the body.

It is not a question of right or wrong. It is more of a question "Does the concept serve us"?

Does it serve us?

This concept will give us a very painful experience because we can never succeed. We can never keep our bodies going forever.

So this concept is no good?

It is worse than no good because if we see we are the body only, then the death of the body is also the death of our beings.

There is no life after death.

Exactly and this will kill us!

You mean death will kill us.

I mean the concept will kill us.

So is there a living concept?

Believe we are souls and not bodies.

Sounds like you are repeating yourself.

Yes, I'm because this concept is so important. If we believe we are souls and they live forever, then we don't have to be too concerned with the death of our bodies.

Why?

Because the death of our bodies does not mean the end of our beings. In fact the death of bodies has nothing to do with our beings because our souls live on with or without bodies.

So, there is life after death.

Exactly! The two concepts are diametrically opposite in consequence.

But how will that help us to live our daily lives?

If you believe we are bodies only, we will treat our bodies as masters, and for every day of our lives, we will serve only our bodies.

I thought that is what everybody does, what is wrong with that?

We will become slaves to our bodies, and we will die as slaves.

You mean we can be masters.

Of course.

How?

By believing we are souls.

Okay.

If we believe we are souls, we will not serve our bodies endlessly because we know that they will die while our souls will live forever. So it'll be much better to serve the interests of the souls rather than the interests of the bodies.

Yes, that makes sense, but how will it help us in our daily lives?

We will focus on our souls and get our bodies to serve the interests of our souls.

How?

We can use our bodies to remind us that we are souls. We can use our bodies to do prayers, meditations, read spiritual texts, listen to spiritual talks and sing spiritual songs.

That sounds good.

Extremely! In fact, by living as souls, we won't be indulging into the pleasures of the bodily senses because we will experience spiritual inner bliss which is far more enjoyable.

Far more blissful.

By living as souls, we will also not be too concerned with the bodily needs; instead we will be more concerned with the evolution of the souls.

Splendid, Guru Harry! We are free from the bodily needs, but what is the evolution of the soul?

To merge with the Divine.

But we are already divine, so we merge with ourselves?

Yes, you are right. Then, let's say to realize we are divine.

Self-realization.

Yes, one of main reasons why we are here on Earth is to realize that we are divine.

Yes, I know we are divine.

How do you know?

You told me so.

Yes, that is external knowing but you need the inner knowing.

What is inner knowing?

To know it by your inner experience without anyone telling you.

What is inner experience?

Spiritual experience such as meditation.

Be still and know that you are god.

Yes, you are god, still or not still.

Yes, you are still god whether you know it or not.

You are god. Amen.

So we are going spiritual?

Souls are spirits.

So by believing or knowing that we are souls, how will that help us in our daily lives?

We can see everyone as souls rather than bodies.

Okay, then?

We don't differentiate ourselves with others by the differences in our bodies.

You mean we don't differentiate ourselves by different races.

Right, there is only one race and that is the human race.

No more "us and them".

We see everyone as souls, and we are all the same.

We look for sameness rather than differences.

Yes, it is like we are all air and there is only one air covering the entire Earth.

We are all one.

We are all connected; so we look for cooperation rather than competition.

Your gain is my gain, and your loss is my loss.

We look for win-win solutions rather than "I win and you lose" scenarios.

So we are all winners.

Wouldn't life be better this way?

Better? It'll be heaven on Earth.

Didn't I tell you so?

That'll be wonderful.

You mean one-derful!

Can you elaborate further on living as souls?

As we live as souls and we know that souls' existence is eternal, we are not too interested in undertaking tasks that are merely for the sustenance of our bodies.

So, life is not about working for a living?

It should not be, but unfortunately many do and life becomes a meaningless struggle.

Meaningless, why meaningless?

Because many struggle just to keep their bodies going and yet their bodies are bound to perish. That is why it is meaningless.

Can we make life more meaningful?

Sure, by undertaking tasks that is good for the soul.

Such as?

To know spiritual truths, and to live with these truths and discriminate against falsehood.

Name one spiritual truth.

We are souls and not bodies.

Can you tell me more about living as souls?

By living as souls, we are not too motivated by physical rewards. That is why we can live with no attachment to physical objects.

This no attachment part, is it really achievable?

It is not a question whether it is achievable. It must be achieved in order to avoid pain.

Attachment leads to pain.

Yes, actually this saying only applies to physical and emotional attachments.

You mean there is a type of attachment that can bring joy?

Yes, by attaching to the Divine, it actually brings bliss. It is called spiritual attachment.

Okay, why do physical and emotional attachments bring us pain?

You see after we take up a body, everyday of our life, we walk with the body, we sit with the body, we talk with the body, we eat with the body and we sleep with the body.

Yes.

So we spend every minute of our life with the body.

Yes.

So, we are very close to the body. In fact, there is no other physical object that can be closer, right?

Right.

Yet on the day we die, can we bring the body with us?

No, actually that is the definition of death.

Then, can we bring other objects that are external to the body?

Since we can't bring the body, how can we bring objects that are external to the body?

That is the cause of pain. We are attached to objects and yet we can't keep them. In fact, we are bound to lose them - sooner or later, and the latest time is the moment of death.

How sad?

We don't have to. We can actually feel peaceful by simply being non-attached to these objects before we lose them.

How can we be non-attached to objects?

Realize that everything we "own" actually doesn't belong to us. They may be temporarily under our care but sooner or later, the ownership will be transferred.

Okay!

So if we don't "own" anything, can we lose anything?

So we can enjoy what we have, and when we lose them, we don't feel pain.

Pleasure without pain.

But they say "pleasure is an interval between two pains"?

After we remove pain, there is only pleasure left, right?

Right. What a wonderful way to live?

Life is meant to be wonderful.

I was told that life is suffering.

Life is only suffering if we believe we are bodies, and we need to keep them going forever.

I was also told that life is a struggle.

Life is only a struggle because the world operates on the basis of competition rather than cooperation.

Can you elaborate?

You see like you and I, if we take a walk on the basis of cooperation, then we will walk at a pace that both of us are comfortable with. We can then also enjoy the scenery on the way.

Enjoy life.

So, who is the winner?

We are both winners.

But if we take the walk on the basis of competition, then we will walk as fast as we can. Both of us will find the walk a struggle and there is no chance to enjoy the scenery.

Life becomes a struggle.

So, who is the winner?

There is no winner, we are both losers.

Exactly, in the world of competitions, even winners are actually losers. That is why the world is full of losers.

And that includes the rich and powerful?

And that includes the rich and powerful!

By believing we are souls, we turn a lose-lose situation to a win-win situation.

By believing we are souls, we bring heaven to Earth.

How about emotional attachment?

This type of attachment can be even more painful.

Why?

Because it is to do with relationships.

Relationships with what?

Relationships with fellow human beings, with animals and even with the environment.

I thought relationships give us pleasure.

Yes, they do.

Then?

Unless we are attached to them.

How can we be non-attached to relationships?

Realize that all relationships are temporal, that is they have a beginning and an end.

You mean we can't have an everlasting relationship?

Actually, there is one relationship we can keep forever.

Oh, that is good. What is that?

Relationship with the Divine.

So apart from the relationship with the Divine and knowing that all other relationships are temporal, will that remove the pain?

Not quite. We also need to know that we don't "own" our children, our animals and our environment.

So we don't own anything, and are non-attached to everything?

Only if you want to experience joy without pain.

Of course we do, but what will life be like by being non-attached to everything?

It'll be heaven on Earth.

I was told that to bring heaven to Earth is to own everything.

Who told you that?

The rich and powerful.

There are many misguided souls on our planet.

How then can we bring heaven to Earth?

By being non-attached to everything.

Okay, how will that affect our daily life?

We can then live a life of renunciation.

I thought a life of renunciation means living in a forest or up in a mountain. Can we really live a life of renunciation when we are in our worldly society?

Right, many think that renunciation means giving up everything, going to a forest or a mountain.

You mean it is not?

Renunciation actually means living without attachment which is being non-attached to everything.

So we can't "own" physical objects?

We may temporarily possess them, and the test is when we lose them, do we feel pain?

If we don't own these objects, there'll be no pain.

You are learning young man! By living beyond gain and loss, we can actually live a life of equanimity.

Is there any other thing that can cause us pain?

Expectations.

What do you mean?

When we take up a body, life actually promises us nothing.

What do you mean?

As an example, when we took up a body, life never promised us how long it would last.

It didn't?

So it may last for 20 years.

Then?

We may feel disappointed.

You mean we shouldn't feel disappointed?

Life will last as long as it'll last. So why should we feel disappointed?

So, why do we feel disappointed?

Because we have been taught to expect life to last around 80 years and when it doesn't, we feel disappointed.

Life is short.

But if we don't have the expectations, then there is no disappointment.

So disappointment is caused by expectations, and not by the actual happening.

Right, disappointment comes when we compare a happening with some reference point.

Remove the reference point, then there is no disappointment.

Exactly, without expectations, we will just observe whatever happens is whatever happens.

That is what the masters do, right?

That is what the masters do.

So what is happening?

Life will last as long as it'll last, and it is better to live without expectations.

Live life with no expectations.

Excellent! Attachments and expectations are the two main causes of sorrow and pain.

So, living without attachments and expectations will bring joy and happiness?

Actually, it'll bring peace.

I thought one main goal in life is to be happy.

Happiness is really a commercial goal, that is why we have "Happy New Year", "Happy Birthday" and so on.

Can you elaborate?

In the commercial world, their business is to sell you things, right?

Right.

It'll be much easier for them to sell if they can convince you that happiness is your main goal in life and their product can bring you happiness.

You mean they don't.

Some products do but whatever happiness they bring, it is only temporal. In fact, it can be very short.

Is there a better goal in life?

Peace.

I thought peace is to do with dying, like "rest in peace".

How about "live in peace"?

Yes, how will peace affect the living?

Suppose shopping makes you happy, but you don't have money. What will you do?

I can work, earn some money and then do my shopping.

Let's say you don't like to work and in any case, you want your money fast. How can you get it?

Steal?

Yes. If happiness is your goal, you can justify stealing because by stealing, you will get your money and after you got your money, you can do your shopping and you will be happy.

But what happens if I'm caught.

This is the man-made law part. So, you can take your chance because you may or may not get caught.

How will it be different if peace is the goal?

If peace is your goal, then you can't justify stealing because getting your money through stealing won't make you feel peaceful.

Can I steal and pretend to be peaceful?

Peace belongs to divine laws. So you can't escape the consequence.

So, I can't rest in peace?

You can, by not stealing!

But I want to be happy?

Yes, there's another problem with happiness as the goal.

What is that?

It leads to immorality.

I was told that it is better to be rich and immoral than poor and moral.

Who told you that?

The rich and powerful.

Exactly, if happiness is your goal, you will conclude that it is better to be rich and immoral.

What happens if peace is my goal?

Then you will conclude that it is better to be poor and moral.

But I was told that morality is a problem because it leads people to sufferings.

Let me ask you a question. Wealth, health and morality, which one is most important?

From the perspective of the rich and powerful, they will say wealth.

Can you bring wealth with you after the body is gone?

No.

Can you bring health with you after the body is gone?

No.

Can you bring morality with you after the body is gone?

This one, I'm not sure. Maybe, maybe not.

Okay, will morality be left somewhere after the body is gone?

You mean it could be attached to the name after the body is gone?

Very good. With good morality, you can leave a good name.

Forever and a day!

There is a saying you know.

What is it?

If you lose your wealth, you lose nothing. If you lose your health, you lose something. If you lose your morality, you lose everything.

So morality is the most important.

Never trade your morality for wealth.

Yes sir, but how about the suffering part?

You see with all the masters who have walked on Earth, did they suffer?

Many of them had to endure terrible physical conditions.

Right, but did they consider them as sufferings?

As they are divine beings, they chose or created those conditions, so they didn't consider them as sufferings.

Splendid! In fact, their divinity shone brightest when they were under those terrible physical conditions.

Yes, those terrible physical conditions actually enhanced their divinity.

So does morality bring sufferings?

Not really. Can we get back to peace?

Yes, we should bring peace back to Earth.

If peace is so good, why don't they promote it?

Because it has little commercial value.

Can you elaborate?

You see peace is a spiritual quality, so we don't need to buy commercial products to achieve peace. In fact if peace is our goal, we will have less desire and we will buy less.

Less luggage, more comfort.

And more peace.

So, what is the problem?

Actually, it is the solution, and there is no problem.

Then?

But our societies measure their success by economic growth.

Everybody measures their success by economic growth, right?

Only in materialistic societies. In spiritual societies, they don't.

How do they measure success?

By physical and spiritual well being of their citizens.

But if we don't have economic growth, we don't grow?

What doesn't grow?

We don't grow because if we don't have economic growth, we don't have jobs, we don't have money, so we can't feed ourselves.

So we need jobs to feed ourselves?

Of course.

How about we use food to feed ourselves?

Yes, we feed ourselves with food, but we need money to buy food, so we need jobs.

How about we focus on producing food rather than jobs?

That is a novel idea!

How about we solve the problem by hitting the hammer on the nail? We just concentrate on producing food?

That is a novel idea, too!

Do you think we can produce enough food for everyone?

Sure, it is a piece of cake.

So we can have our cake and eat it.

We can all eat it.

So there'll be no hunger in this world.

A world free of hunger.

How about we do the same on clothing and housing?

You mean we concentrate on producing enough clothing and housing for everyone?

Do you think it can be done?

Since we can produce enough weapons to decimate the planet many times over, surely we can produce enough clothing and housing for everyone.

So what will happen when all the basic human needs are satisfied?

Joy to the world.

Hallelujah!

And peace on Earth.

Yes, there is another important aspect of peace.

What is that?

Only after we have attained peace then we can practice love.

Love all, serve all!

How many people practice this?

Very few and far between.

Why?

Because we don't have peace?

May you have peace!

If peace is so important, why is it not happening?

Maybe we are focusing on the wrong things?

Like economic growth?

Do we need economic growth?

Sounds quite irrelevant when all our basic needs are satisfied.

In fact, there is another problem with economic growth?

What is that?

It is not sustainable.

Why not?

Economic growth relies on more and more consumption but the world's resources are finite.

So it is against the laws of nature?

It is a losing strategy.

Anything that is against the laws of nature is doomed to failure?

Actually, it is already a proven failure.

Really?

For the past few decades, the world has experienced unprecedented economic growth.

Then?

Do we still have poverty on Earth?

Yes, we do. How can we save the world?

Change the focus.

Focus to what?

Physical and spiritual well being of the citizens.

How?

Provide basic physical needs and then let them evolve spiritually.

Sounds like heaven on Earth.

Yes, we can transform Earth into heaven.

Chapter 4

Conversation with Guru Harry (Part 2)

Are there other benefits by living as souls?

Plenty.

What are they?

If we believe we are souls, we can then leave one body and subsequently take up another. We may consider bodies are like clothes which we wear one for one day, and then change to another on another day.

Reincarnation.

Correct and there is a huge benefit in this belief.

What is that?

We are not attached to our bodies.

We are souls and not bodies.

By being non-attached from the body, we gain enormous power.

What power?

By living as the soul and having a body, we always have the option of leaving the body.

So?

Since we have the power to leave the body, it also means that if we decide to stay with the body, it is our own choice.

We are empowered to leave or to stay.

It means that whatever situation we are in, we choose to be there.

Right on.

It means that nobody in the entire universe can make us do what we don't want.

We don't have to do what we don't want.

Since everything we do is our own choosing, we become masters of life.

Congratulations!

There are other advantages in becoming masters of life.

What are they?

Since whatever action we take is of our own choosing, our actions are empowered. Since we are empowered, whatever task that we undertake, we will do it with conviction, and bear the responsibility. We won't blame others for the consequence. By fully accepting the consequence of our own action, we can live a life of peace and no regret.

So peace at last.

So by believing we are bodies, we are slaves of life, and by believing we are souls, we are masters of life.

So getting the "right" belief is very important because they give diametrically opposite outcomes.

Absolutely, but getting the "right" belief should not be a problem because we are completely free to choose what we like to believe.

But how come so many people live their lives as slaves?

Because they have been taught the "wrong" belief.

Who taught them?

Society leaders.

How come they teach people the "wrong" belief?

Because they have been taught the "wrong" belief.

Who taught them?

Society leaders.

You mean we have been taught the "wrong" belief for generations.

Generations after generations.

How come?

Because societies measure their success by economic growth.

So, it is the "wrong" focus?

It is only wrong in the sense that it will lead people to live a hard life rather than a joyful life.

I thought economic growth is meant to lead people to a joyful life?

For the past few decades, the world has experienced unprecedented economic growth. Are people joyful?

Some are, but most are miserable.

Then, change the focus.

Focus to what?

Physical and spiritual well being of the citizens.

Will living as souls help us to be joyful?

Sure, you see bodies have many needs just to keep them going, while souls don't have any and they live forever. So by living as souls, we can live a life of no needs.

You mean we can live with nothing?

At the soulful level, we can and we should because there isn't any needs. There is another great advantage in living a life of no needs.

What is that?

We can freely choose where to live and what to do.

Freedom at last!

Wouldn't you say that is "real" freedom?

So we don't need any physical objects or relationships.

No physical and emotional attachments.

A life without attachments!

Wouldn't it be joyful then?

It'll be blissful.

Yes, we can have heaven on Earth.

Are there any other beliefs that can help us?

Believe that there is a Great Spirit.

What is that?

This is a non-physical entity and has great power. It is inside us, outside us, above us, below us, in front of us and behind us. It is also inside every being, every plant and all physical and non-physical objects. It is larger than the universe and smaller than an atom. It is everywhere and yet appears nowhere.

Sounds like you are talking about the Divine.

You are right. Great Spirit is Divine.

Then, why do you call it by a different name?

It is to move away from a common "misconception" of the Divine.

Which is?

The Divine is external to us and resides in some faraway place.

Like Heaven?

Exactly! Many are taught that Heaven is some faraway place and we can only get there during our afterlife.

You mean it is not true?

I mean a "better" concept to teach is to say heaven can be on Earth during our present life, right here right now.

Is heaven on Earth right now?

Well, with the new concept, we can transform Earth into heaven.

Guru Harry, there are still many contradictions in your description of the Great Spirit.

Actually there are no contradictions. You only perceive them as contradictions because you see it from the physical viewpoint.

Can you explain?

The Great Spirit is of course a spiritual entity and so it follows the spiritual laws. There are things that can't occur under physical laws but they can occur under spiritual laws. When these things happen, we call them "miracles".

I love miracles.

Miracles happen all the time.

Really?

You see whenever there are inconsistencies between the physical and spiritual laws, spiritual laws prevail and miracles happen.

I thought miracles are created by the Divine.

In a way they are, because both physical and spiritual laws are divine laws.

So what else should we know about the Great Spirit?

The Great Spirit has great spiritual power, and since the Great Spirit is inside us, we too have this great spiritual power.

So this spiritual power is not outside us, it is within us.

Also, believe that this Great Spirit will only do us good.

How?

Believe that we and the Great Spirit are one.

We are all one.

Then, it is only logical that the Great Spirit will only do us good because whatever is good for us, it is good for the Great Spirit.

It'll be great living with such a Great Spirit.

Absolutely, and living with the Great Spirit, we won't feel lonely anymore.

Alone without loneliness.

That is how masters live, right?

Right, they can live alone for many years.

And no need for social life.

How else will living with this Great Spirit help us in our daily life?

Since we know the Great Spirit is on our side, whatever task we undertake, we will do our best and leave the outcome to the Great Spirit.

We will surrender to the Great Spirit and let the Great Spirit determine the outcome.

We can then live a life of letting go.

Let go and let God!

This will also transform us to see "bad" events as "good" events.

There are no good or bad, only thinking makes it so.

We will see "bad" events as learning events. So we can live in peace.

Peace and equanimity.

We can then live a life without fear.

We will dare to face more challenges.

We will dare to go outside our comfort zone.

The whole world becomes one comfort zone.

This will be truly heaven on Earth!

Hallelujah!

Yes, in fact this is the way to love.

Which way?

If we believe we are souls, connected to all beings and have no need, then we can live a life of non-attachment, honesty, love and compassion.

We will become loving beings.

There will be only love and no more sin.

We will not sin because if we cheat others, we cheat ourselves.

We will live in truth and demonstrate that by being consistent in thought, word and deed.

How wonderful if everyone behaves like this?

How wonderful if we behave like this?

You mean we should take the lead and be an example.

Lead by example!

How else should we live our lives?

We should live as masters and come back in a body to help others.

I was told that we don't help any-body.

To help others is another main reason why we are here.

Help ever, hurt never!

Yes, we should never harm another - be it a human, an animal or the environment.

So, we should become vegetarians?

Will it do less harm to animals?

Not only animals, it will also do less harm to the environment.

It will help to reduce global warming.

The world will become a cooler place to live.

The world will become a better place to live.

How else should we live our lives?

We should live a selfless and egoless life.

How to be egoless?

Attribute all successes to the Great Spirit. Know that we are only instruments.

Does ego serve a purpose?

You see ego is to do with the identity "I". So, if you have done a piece of work and your name is on it, how would you feel?

I've done it!

Is the quality good?

Of course it is good because everyone knows that it is done by me.

For the same piece of work but now your name isn't on it, is the quality good?

It may not be because even if it is poor, nobody knows that it is done by me.

So, ego promotes quality of work.

It makes us more responsible.

Without ego, we may be responsible, but with ego, we will be more responsible.

So ego serves a purpose.

Everything created by the Divine has a purpose.

But there is a negative side to ego, right?

Right. It is like a knife, it can be used to save a life or it can be used to end a life.

So, we just use the positive side of ego and leave the negative side untouched.

Then, we will become an egoless ego!

So, everything that has been programmed into the computer game has a purpose.

Yes, everything in the game of life has a purpose and we can play it as many times as we like.

Because we can have bodies after bodies.

That is why the concept of reincarnation is so important.

What happens when we played the game and we lose?

Winning and losing in the game of life are actually illusions, just like in a computer game. So they are not important. What is important is that the more often we play, the better we become.

We become better players in the game of life.

We become a more humane being and a more enlightened soul.

Can we change the subject to education?

Sure, we all need a good education.

You mean you are in favor of good education?

I'm in favor of all things good and beautiful.

That includes playing computer games?

That includes playing the game of life.

What do you think of the present education system?

It is too long and there is a serious problem.

What is the problem?

It doesn't educate students to become more humane beings and more enlightened souls.

Is it supposed to?

The end product of education should be students of good character, and have an enlightened mind.

So, what is the present system producing?

Students with book knowledge and some worldly skills.

Aren't these useful when looking for jobs?

Education should be more than looking for jobs.

What should it be?

Educate students to become more humane beings and more enlightened souls.

Yes, you have said that before. How?

Spiritual education.

Like what is said in this conversation?

Like what is said in this conversation.

But spiritual education is meant to be taught in religious organizations, and not in schools of a secular society.

There are many misguided souls on our planet.

So, how should it be?

First seek the kingdom of god.

How does this apply to education?

Learn spirituality first, and then worldly matters.

But you said the present education system is already too long?

Cut down the subjects on worldly matters.

But they need these subjects to get jobs.

Do you know how much a person learns is actually applied in jobs?

No, I don't.

Well, let me put it this way. The spirituality they learn, they can apply it everyday of their life, but I can't say the same about the worldly matters.

So, how much of the worldly matters they have learnt is actually applied in jobs?

For advanced level of learning, that may not be much.

The more they learn, the less they use.

In fact for the advanced level of learning, it is about learning more and more about less and less.

Until they learn everything about nothing.

Then, we call them specialists.

How did the system end up this way?

Because it benefits the person who came up with the system.

What is the benefit?

The longer the education duration, more students he will get, so it means more money and power for him.

What is the remedy?

Make the education system shorter and let the students start work earlier.

Then?

They learn while they work.

Sounds like the old apprenticeship system.

It is a better system because what they learn is not just book knowledge; it is backed up by work experience. Also, they don't study just for examinations. They study because they need to learn the skills that they can apply in their jobs.

So, the entire education system has to be revamped?

Only if you want a "meaningful" education system.

Apart from the education system, what else do you think is a major problem in the world today?

World leaders.

I thought the major problems today are terrorists and global warming.

These are the side-effects of the major problems.

Can you explain?

Why do you think terrorists do what they do?

Because they want to make certain changes to the world?

Right, but it is not right for them to use violence as a means to achieve their ends, is it?

No, it is not. In fact, it is terrible!

But do you observe one thing about the terrorists?

What is that?

The terrorists think like the terrorists, talk like the terrorists, and do what terrorists do.

They are consistent in their thoughts, words and deeds.

Splendid! Can you say the same thing about the world leaders?

I would like to but I don't think I can.

That is why it is so important for the world leaders also to be consistent in their thoughts, words and deeds.

You mean they are not?

You see what they do to the terrorists.

An eye for an eye. A tooth for a tooth.

Right, but it is not right for them to use violence as a means to achieve their ends, is it?

You mean it is not right to use violence to achieve peace?

You can't use violence to achieve peace.

I thought everyone is doing it.

That is why there is no peace.

No peace on Earth!

In fact, we are probably still within the most violent period of human history.

How about global warming?

What is the cause of global warming?

The scientists tell us that it is due to burning of fossil fuel.

Why do we burn fossil fuel?

To generate energy.

Why do we generate energy?

Partly for domestic consumption, but mainly for industrial consumption.

Why do industries consume energy?

To produce goods and services.

Why do they produce goods and services?

To make profit and in a larger picture, to achieve economic growth.

I see. So where is the problem?

But still how can we avert global warming?

If economic growth is the cause, move away from economic growth.

How?

Consume less?

We can't do that because we need all the goods and services.

How about luxury items?

Some people want them.

Who?

The rich and powerful.

Do they need them?

It is not a question of need. Luxury items are good because they make some people richer.

And the world poorer!

Who cares?

Yes, this is the other cause of global warming.

What is that?

You know we said we should practice "we are all one".

Yes.

Well, that includes the environment.

So?

So we should live in harmony with the environment.

What happens if you don't?

The environment operates under the divine laws. If we work against the laws, we are bound to get a reaction.

Like global warming?

Like global warming.

Yes, can we get back to the major problem mentioned by you which is world leaders?

Sure.

What is the problem?

As I said before, they are not consistent in their thoughts, words and deeds.

How can you tell?

You see there are people dying of hunger on our planet.

Yes, I do.

This problem has been around for many generations.

Yes.

Why do you think the world is in such a state?

I thought the problem is too large and complicated. So it takes time to sort it out.

But the problem has been around for generations, and actually there is sufficient food for all. Don't you think we should have sorted it out by now?

Yes, one would imagine so.

So, why isn't it sorted out?

Because nobody is doing it?

Right, because all the leaders are only looking after their own interests.

They are?

There is one more sobering thought.

What is it?

Are the leaders really performing when there is still hunger on Earth?

Are they?

You see for the survival of human body, food is the most basic need.

Most basic.

So an easy way to tell the performance of leaders is to see whether there is hunger at the bottom stratum of society.

Look at the bottom and not the top.

Top and bottom, we are all one.

You mean they don't practice "we are all one"?

Do they?

So it is "top versus bottom".

Us versus them.

The rich get richer and the poor get poorer.

So, how can we have peace on Earth?

We don't. We only have violence.

Yes, we are probably still within the most violent period of human history.

So how can we change them?

Spiritual education.

But they are so old.

If you educate the young, they'll do good in their present incarnation. If you educate the old, they'll do good in their future incarnations.

So, it is never too late?

It is never too old.

113

Are there other major problems on Earth?

Religion.

I thought religion helps to save humanity.

Yes, they are supposed to but you see, how long has religion been around?

Thousands of years.

Are humans more humane and more enlightened today?

I would like to think so but I can't say they are.

So to put it mildly, they are not effective in what they are doing.

I see your point, but why is this so?

Because today's religion is "fear-based" rather than "love-based".

What do you mean?

You see with the concept of Heaven and Hell. Who goes to Heaven and who goes to Hell?

The "good" go to Heaven, and the "bad" go to Hell.

That is it. This is called fear-based, separatist theology. First, they are saying if you don't do good, you'll go to Hell. So, they are using fear to motivate people to do good. Second, they are dividing people into two groups.

We are all two.

On top of that, there is another problem?

What is that?

What happens if there are no Heaven and no Hell?

Then, we have done good for nothing.

Exactly, that is the problem with today's religion. It is still based on a reward system, and to make it worse, we can't even be certain of the reward.

You mean we shouldn't be rewarded for doing good?

You have said it. We should do good for the sake of doing good, and don't expect any reward, spiritually or otherwise.

So, we should do good out of love.

Love seeks no reward; love is its own reward.

That is what the masters do, right?

That is what the masters do.

But I was encouraged to do good with the concept "As you sow, so you reap".

So you have. Unfortunately, this concept is also not effective because there is an expectation of reward attached to the action.

We should do good and expect nothing in return.

Precisely!

How about charity?

Charity is good if it is true charity.

What is true charity?

True charity is giving without expecting anything in return.

Most people give money to charity, and don't expect any money back, right?

Right, they don't expect money, but they expect something more valuable in return.

What is that?

Reputation.

What reputation?

By giving to charity, they can enhance their reputation by claiming that they are "good".

You mean they are not.

Many corporations give to charity and if you see the type of business they are in, you wouldn't say they are good.

How about individuals?

Yes, many individuals also use charity to enhance their reputation.

So, what happens if they expect something in return?

Then, it is not true charity, it is really a transaction.

Like a business transaction?

Like a business transaction.

Is there another way to motivate people to do good?

Believe that "we are all one".

And we are one with the Great Spirit.

So all of us will end up at the same place.

We are all at the same place.

Exactly, we are all in it together and there is nowhere to go.

We don't need to go anywhere.

This is it.

You mean Earth is heaven.

We can transform Earth into heaven.

It is all up to us?

We are divine. We decide.

Hallelujah!

We have the whole world in our hands.

Then surely, we can transform Earth into heaven.

Yes, we can.

What about family?

What about it?

Is it good to get married and have a family?

Family is the foundation of society. If you can practice and promote love within your family, then you are contributing to bringing peace to Earth.

How about parents?

Yes, what about them?

Should we look after them?

This is the greatest service you can ever do. As they say "Charity begins at home".

But I was advised to dump them?

Well, if you do, is there a greater sin?

But it'll be such a burden? You know anything can happen to these old folks anytime, so we have to be on standby all the time.

Yes, it is a great responsibility to look after your old parents and it is not easy. But if you serve with your heart, it'll become a great joy and not a burden.

Also we are not talking for one or two years. It can be for 10 years or longer, and while we are looking after them, there are many things we can't do?

When you have served your parents for 10 years or longer, you will feel a great sense of fulfillment. Also, when you are given the opportunity to serve that can bring you great joy, why do you want to do other things?

But we never promised to serve them when we were born?

To serve others is another main reason why we are here on Earth. This is the path to god. To serve your parents is of course a top priority.

To god means to be divine?

Yes, this is the path to be divine.

Can we say that by looking after our parents, it will encourage our children to look after us next time?

We should serve our parents without expectation of reward. So we shouldn't impose an expectation on our children whom we bring to the world at our own free will.

How about friends?

Friends are fine if they are good.

How do you tell they are good?

You can ask three questions.

What are they?

First, listen to what they say and then observe what they do. Are their words consistent with their deeds?

Okay, consistency in words and deeds because we can't see their thoughts.

Second, observe their company. Are they good?

Yes, we can tell what the person is like by his associations.

Third, observe how they treat people who will never bring them any benefit. Are they humane?

Yes, we will usually treat people well if they can bring us some benefit, but to those who can't, we may not treat them well.

Like the old, poor and powerless.

Yes, like the old, poor and powerless.

If the answers to all three questions are yes, they are good.

What happens if we can't find good friends?

It is better to have no friends than "bad" friends.

No company is better than "bad" company.

In fact, there is one great advantage in having no company.

What is that?

More time for God.

Guru Harry, is there anything else you would like to talk about?

Well, it has been a long chat. Maybe I'll take a rest now, but I'll leave you one article. It is a letter I wrote to my son advising him on his working life. It can be found in Appendix B.

Guru Harry, thank you very much. Maybe I won't have a chance to see you again before you go.

That is alright, Tom.

May you rest in peace, Guru Harry!

I will, and there is one more thing.

What is that?

After I've left my body, there is no need to grieve.

Why?

Remember everything in life, it is our own choosing.

Yes, I remember.

So our soul chooses when and where to take up a body, and also when and where to leave the body.

Okay.

In fact there is no need to grieve for any-body because they are all leaving their bodies at a time and place of their own choosing.

Then, I won't grieve but I'll pray for them.

Amen.

Well, thank you for all the spiritual wisdom. Although you are not considered a success in our society, seeing the peace and divinity in you, I'm sure what you have said is right.

Goodbye, Tom!

Goodbye, Guru Harry!

Appendix A

Who Am I?

This question is of monumental importance because if the answer is "I am the body," we will live our lives one way. If the answer is "I am not the body," we will live our lives in a completely different way. This article examines whether it is wise to identify ourselves with the body.

If somebody asked me "Who am I?" By this society's convention, I'll probably give the following answers:

(1)   I'm Harry,
(2)   I'm 89 years old,
(3)   I'm 1.7 m tall,
(4)   I weigh 65 kg,
(5)   I'm a Singaporean,
(6)   I'm a lecturer,
(7)   I teach,
(8)   I live in a house,
(9)   I drive a Japanese car,
(10) I've one thousand two hundred and thirty-four dollars,

(11) I like reading spiritual books, and

(12) I support a football team called Arsenal.

These twelve points appear to comprehensively describe who I am. Now let's examine them point by point:

(1) this is the name for the body and it can be changed,

(2) this is the age of the body and it changes every year,

(3) this is the height of the body and it changes,

(4) this is the weight of the body and it changes,

(5) this is the nationality of the body and it can be changed,

(6) this is the amount of money owned by the body and it can change - by the minute,

(7) this is the job title for the body and it can be changed,

(8) this is the job function of the body and it can be changed,

(9) this is where the body lives and it can be changed,

(10) this is the car driven by the body and it can be changed,

(11) this is a liking of the body and it can be changed,

(12) this is the football team supported by the body and out of all the points, this is the only one that can never change – ha ha!

So it appears that everything to do with the body changes. In fact, our body keeps on changing and eventually, it disintegrates and reduces to ashes. So is it wise to identify ourselves with the body?

Who am I?

Appendix B

Working Life

My Dear Son

My advice to your working life is:

Choose a job that is in keeping with your *interest*. Choose a career that is in keeping with your *mission*.

If you choose to work in the public sector, don't let the authority that you may possess blind you.

If you choose to work in the private sector, don't let the monetary reward that you may receive blind you.

Above all, be human.
That is *be humane, be compassionate, be love.*

Serve God by serving men.
Be God, be a "light" to the world.

May you have a successful working life.
That is *a meaningful and fulfilling life.*

May God bless you!

Dad

Index

About the author

As a bestselling author on Amazon, Dr. Tommy Wong is a civil engineer by training, and an award-winning hydrologist. Having lived a worldly life, he now lives spiritually in the midst of modern Singapore. Nowadays, he serves the world as a freelance consultant and trainer. He is also an editor and has authored books of four different genres: engineering, philosophy, self-help and spirituality.

Since 2009, his books have been available on Amazon and many other online bookstores worldwide. In 2012, 2013 and 2017, he was featured on the Radio 938LIVE programme "A Slice of Life Hour". He has also given talks at the Singapore Writers Festival, Heartlands Book Club, Booktique bookstore, Financial Services Consumer Association, as well as various Meetup groups. Further information about Dr. Wong's work can be found on his website http://wisdomlife.page4.me/ and the FB page https://www.facebook.com/wisdomlivelife.

Selected books by Tommy S. W. Wong

Wong, T.S.W. (2009) "How Sai Baba Attracts Without Direct Contact," CrcatcSpacc, North Charleston, USΛ, 108 pp.

Wong, T.S.W. (2010) "Wisdom on How to Live Life," CreateSpace, North Charleston, USA, 156 pp.

Wong, T.S.W. (2010) "Wisdom on How to Live Life (Book 2)," CreateSpace, North Charleston, USA, 110 pp.

Wong, T.S.W. (2010) "Wisdom on How to Live Life (Book 3)," CreateSpace, North Charleston, USA, 124 pp.

Wong, T.S.W. (2011) "How Sai Baba Attracts Without Direct Contact (Book 2)," CreateSpace, North Charleston, USA, 102 pp.

Wong, T.S.W. (2011) "Wisdom on How to Live Life (Book 4)," CreateSpace, North Charleston, USA, 122 pp.

Wong, T.S.W. (2012) "Minimum Wage for Low Wage Workers," CreateSpace, North Charleston, USA, 42 pp.

Wong, T.S.W. (2012) "Wisdom for Spiritual Living," CreateSpace, North Charleston, USA, 134 pp.

Wong, T.S.W. (2012) "Wisdom on How to Live Life (Book 5)," CreateSpace, North Charleston, USA, 134 pp.

Wong, T.S.W. (2013) "Masters of Life on Meaningful Living," CreateSpace, North Charleston, USA, 136 pp.

Wong, T.S.W. (2013) "Wisdom for End-of-Life Living," CreateSpace, North Charleston, USA, 62 pp.

Wong, T.S.W. (2014) "Masters of Life on Good Life and Good Society," CreateSpace, North Charleston, USA, 146 pp.

Wong, T.S.W. (2014) "Wisdom for Living After Being Fired," CreateSpace, North Charleston, USA, 70 pp.

Wong, T.S.W. (2015) "Wisdom for Living as Spiritual Beings," CreateSpace, North Charleston, USA, 160 pp.

Wong, T.S.W. (2016) "How an Engineering Professor Becomes a Spiritual Philosopher," CreateSpace, North Charleston, USA, 164 pp.

Wong, T.S.W. (2016) "Wisdom for Living as Spiritual Masters," CreateSpace, North Charleston, USA, 150 pp.

Wong, T.S.W. (2017) ""Wisdom on How to Live Life" Quotations," CreateSpace, North Charleston, USA, 64 pp.